Gemini Blood Moon

Shelby Stephens

BookLeaf
Publishing

India | USA | UK

Presentation by *BookLeaf Publishing*

Web: www.bookleafpub.com

E-mail: info@bookleafpub.com

ISBN: 9789357211659

First edition 2023

DEDICATION

Grazie, bella mia Phia.

Thank you, *A.* You'll never know what you did for me. You have allowed me to become beyond.

ACKNOWLEDGEMENT

Editor: Liliana Urso

Thank you…
… the stitches in your chin were not my fault…
…but you introduced us so I wouldn't have had the experiences to stain this paper with, if it wasn't for you. Truly, thank you.

~ **Eight/Eleven/TwentyTwo** ~

Your presence is only present in moments.
For the time it takes those two shakes
Of the sacrificial lamb's tail
We have been killed.
Despite the duration, in these moments you still
Consume my entire being,
You can move me, I sway to the melody the
Wind plays through your hair.
Before you disappear back out to sea.
It's our waves.

You are a welcomed
Rupture to my gravity.
You live above and out of my reach,
But not far enough, your hold, immaterially Felt.
These are our waves.

You always held my tears and tides,
Even when clouds of uncertainty obscure,
Crossing,
Without looking twice,
My mind.

Even through the nights
When my sky is vibrant with someone else,

I will witness your presence in the waking blue
Of morning,
Waiting till my gaze catches yours.
To pull me once again.
These are the moments that pass too fast.
No time to play
'COME BACK TO EARTH'
As the sun scatters you,
Out of sight
Almost without sound.

You are the soul to show me serenity.

You shone sacredly last night.
Your force held course while my
Transfixed gaze remembers how my eyes
Came to know what is meant by
Divine beauty.

~ **No Vacancy** ~

There are nights Her & He hold each other.
The way his hair is gripped within Her hold,
The way Her nails trace constellations into his
Soul's cast,
The way Her breath is enclosed between the
Embrace of their lips,
& hips.
But not their hearts.

He recognises the beauty she is finding in
another.
True beauty is peripheral and moving into focus.
She will regret the waste
The morbid waste of all that they have (left)
Time.

The heart Her's is halting for will show Her all
She is deserved,
Being divine as she is.

He knows this pleasurable exchange will expire
At the reward of Her metamorphosis.

From hope to being held: Her heart will know
Why it let Her fall again

Despite the last cliff edge that crumbled beneath
Her.

Her and He share the hearts akin.
Both without vacancy for another,
Yet, Her peripherals are turning her towards a
Future,
While He lives within himself,
Longing
For one long lost.

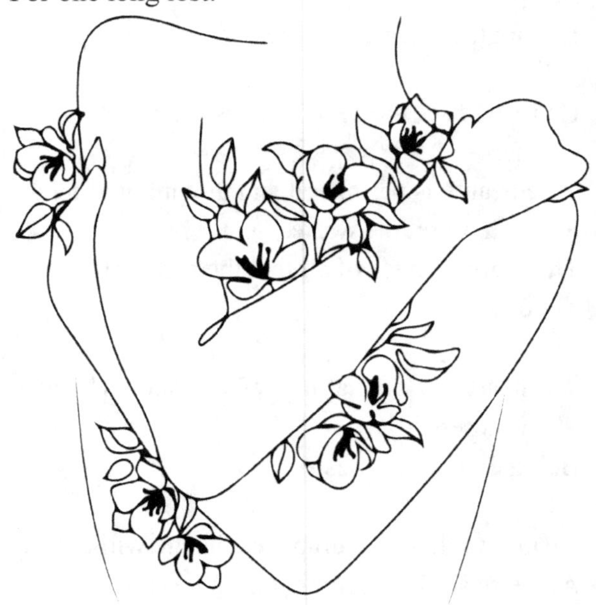

~ **Separate Studies** ~

4:04 15-11-22
You sit a moment away from me in this booth.

We are only here to produce productivity.
From the remnants of the comfortable silence
We perfected a certain lifetime previously.
Alternatively,
Previously perfected in another lifetime
For certain.

You sit, with your burgundy acrylics
Interchanging their...

*a pause should be allowed here as one
enchantingly eloped
as her lips parted,
spilling an invisible liqueur,
potent enough to halt my train of thought in
place,
without derailing a single carriage.
no passenger words were even disturbed*

...Purpose
From curating legislation literature,
The key strikes are melodic as if they were
Aligned

Single file.
White &
Black.
The spacebar, middle C.
&
Entrancing in unison around the cardboard
Chalice of vanilla-soy caffeine
To stimulate a wavering concentration.

These same hands have interwoven themselves
Within my own.
Today my lips are blessed pressing against them.

Breaking a divergent focus held within each
Other's eyes
I return to my page and pen,
As you do to your keyboard and caffeine
But my peripheral view enlightens with the
reflection of wavelengths
Made iridescent by your light.
There's a grin you have seeded the birth of
Across my cheek.
I silently vow to myself to return the favour.

Both hands have crossed my French watchface
Faster than we wished (any movement of time
During the moments spent with you
Is a disgrace against our desires)

You are off to move with grace,
Before you do I leave
A press of my lips against your cheek
& through the lowered window
Our first person perspective of
Three words are said,

A postmodern-romantic protest
Opposing a
Goodbye.

~ **Ode On Scarred Skin** ~

The negative capability inked in my skin,
Has been birthed out of definitive design
& subconscious selection akin.
It appears my heart for-goes resign.

Although the mind emanates from the brain,
It exists in the keratin of fingertips,
The bleeding ink tattooed and the pain
Held within steady grips.

I see us both in the fine line,
The permanent black petals
That will only wilt with the slit of my twine,
& when ashes of my bones settle.

The scarred skin now holds
A cherub, he sees the petals too.
Waiting for the folds
To reveal and guide them to a sacred hue.

I did not ink his life,
Nor fill his lungs with air.
Yet I can see a perspective,
The way he watches the pair.

Let us see them slip and fall.

Watch as they learn to adore.
Witness the resurgence and
Wonder with awe!

Two souls like twins
Of the same flames and sins
Entangled. Entwined.
Without finite, combined

Their shells of skin
Are aware akin
of their ephemeral nature
And time till rupture.

But their hearts knew time
Before dawn knew rhyme
And will keep together
For this episode's endeavour.

Till the day the rains
Water the poppies I sprout.
I will exist there again,
If my name, you ever shout.

Goodmorning ****
I'm still certain of my love,
Even if there is an asymmetrical
Reciprocity.

~ **The Weight** ~

Can you taste the bitterness when you swallow
your words?

Do you feel empty when your tongue let's go of
What had to fall?

How often do you regret the words you spoke?
How often do you regret the words you didn't?
Do you regret them at all?

Which weight is worse?

Internally I sink in my own deafening silence.
When my thoughts return from recess and beat a
Migraine into these unholy temples.

There is more to our story.
Years I yearn to endure.
I feel it as real as the papercuts I suffer,
Illustrating with this ink, page
By page.

But my bleeding thumb leaves my identity
In the distressed wave print.
A chaos only I could leave behind.

What if the story is truly finished–
& the audience has left–
& the lights have burnt out–
What should I make of these words of mine?
What am I to do with all I have not said?

Have I been scripting our epilogue

Alone?

The weight of my words,
Spoken
&
Unheard
Are polarised opposites
on a set of scales
B a l a   n c e d
As they crush me to my knees.

~ **High Tide** ~

High tide, it roars.
It is the before hours of
Morning of a restless night.

He leaves his window wide,
Open despite the winter's bite.

The cold, winter carries never
Did bother the boiling blood in his veins;
But the agony of a
Flame burning out…
Burnt out,
Hold his eye lids up like black balloons.

He writes to her,
Near enough every night,
To her blind eyes
& sings to her severed ears.

This burnt out flame we speak of,
It's not hers.

She burns brighter than the stars that
Embraced her at conception,
The stars that are being felt from worlds aways.

Like the poison of burning tire smoke,
Ashes scatter in the breeze but
Not before staining his fingernails
& the floor…
He doesn't mind.

Feeling lost is the only
Feeling of home he knows anymore,
The two conditioned to be one and the same,
Every wave crashing sounds as loud as
Fireworks
Or tear droplets in the rain.

His dreams extend into legacy,
His printed words staining
The memories of generations.

But he barely can lift the weight of the
Ink to mark his first stroke of a finite potential.

Only finite by the limitations
The limitless universe has inscribed
In the language of the stars.
We call it mathematics.

Sustaining these heavy black balloons are
Potions of unpronounced chemicals
Unnamed, they do their duty
& carry the weight.

His weight.
A weight he cannot carry on his own…

15

~ Swimming ~

Dear Malcolm,

My head is above water now,
But I have found home in the depths,
Where the pressure
Will crush
Your bones
& bury your soul.

I have lived there.
Where they will you to swallow your lungs
& sink your heart.
I know the viscous veins of the trenches.

I will never drown now.

~ **Pleasure Lost** ~

She sees worth in his words.
He values her vows.
She is someone else's even though
He does protest possession.

She marches in solidarity, though it is ironic.
He moves through smoke, his heart belongs to
another.
She stays on call, in view of his craft, these
Words
He writes on the crest of your very lips.

There is no more accommodating
For the body of his worn through soul.

They will continue to discuss the finite things in
life
But as the sun sets She slips into the sheets with
another.
He, aware of this eventuation, is not wounded.
He is whole-less.

She fills her heart each day a little more,
Letting it overflow on occasion.
another has blessed her days
& nights with love deserved.

The shared darkness will not go unremembered,
He holds Her in his mind as tightly as
She pulled him in with her legs around his back.
Together they made a heaven out of their hell.
Now she has escaped the brimstone and
He resides alone.

~ The Fall of Man ~

Rest your broken whiskey glass less than an
Arm's reach.
Rest it aside the brand new phone, destroyed in
That crash.
Sip your unprescribed aliment and attempt
Self-destruction.
Show don't tell.
Show.
She's not Helen Keller even when she does not
Hear.

Feel that burn,
The corrosion to the back of the throat,
The impending liver failure
To bleed out these words.

I don't know how to stop
This love.
This rose thorn piercing me.
Killing unkindly.
I feel your gravity
Like the pain of standing on both bare heels
In the gravel, the ruble and wreckage of
My self destruction.
I still live out the regret of the boy I was.
But the man I am today is still not enough.

Every eighteen minute lapse of change.
I still can't find who I need to be
For you.

I may not ever drown, despite a desire to.
Instead I spend every fleeting moment
Choking on the formulation of a fallen future,
Fabricated from fractured fragments
Of fictional flashbacks.
Fuck.

~ **The Rise of Something Else** ~

Crush the rest of the whiskey glass
In the chamber of your palm.
Let the blood drip into the pages of
Your invasive thoughts,
The alcohol will burn in the cuts.
Sometimes pain's a saviour.

Step outside.
Set mary-jane alight,
Be sure to dry the wound before the sparks
Set ablaze more than intended.
But you do spark more than intended,
You fall back into thought.

Vivid are the visions of that midday
In the dark.
Her lips artificially red,
Like the organic red staining my page.
But her eyes stole my attention,
Draining my being into them.
The purity of calmness
In the neutrality of her cinnamon
Was nothing less than a deception.
I would never come to see her as neutral
Ever again.

She commands vibrance with a smile
& confidence with a head tilt.

That is how
I met my muse.
& I have been bleeding
On these pages
Ever since.

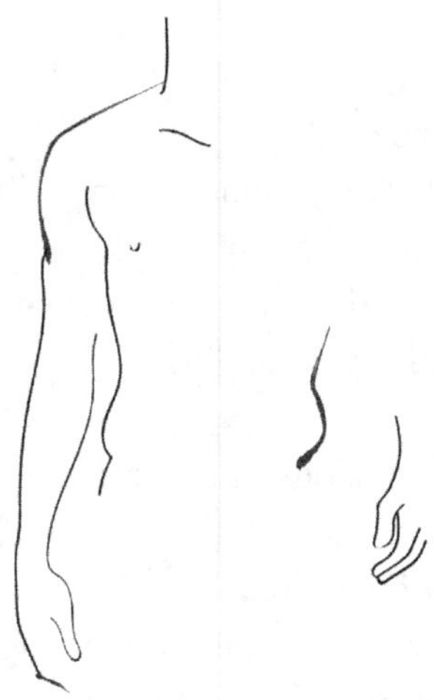

~ **Ash Tray Dreams** ~

Inhale.
Exhale.
I can still taste you.

Inhale.
Exhale.
It has to be nicotine cascading through your
bloodstream.

Lost in a daydream, I'm wide awake while my
neighbours, even their dogs sleep soundlessly.
The smouldering paper between my lips burns
into the filter. It's the artificial flavour of the
futile division that snaps me from seeing you,
there, with me.

Pressing into the ashtray, I fall into last night's
scene.

My lips learn the function of your thighs. Each
burning kiss leaves no mark, other than a
milestone in my memories. In unison, my
fingertips caress your skin. Behind them follows
a trail of goosebumps and tiny hairs searching
for the North Star. Sounding louder than dawn's
crashing waves, I can hear your voice again. The

soft long breathing in my ear. Reliving the night
with the salt air rushing out to sea. I fear your
breaths will be heard too similar to the wind and
the waves. All at once the air is heard and felt,
only to vanish out of reach.
Leaving my seat to have the balcony's glass hold
my weight, I wish I could fall and embrace your
elegance once again. With your chest pressed
against mine, your legs holding me in tight and
the fleeting scent of your perfume wearing thin.

I felt alive in your presence. I felt immortal in its
pleasure. To please you is a blessing, a privilege
I would never tire to receive.
My hands miss the sculpting grip they had over
your thighs and your throat. In all the intimacy I
have swallowed, a simple drop on my tongue of
ours had left me inebriated.

In your bed, I believed I belonged.

~ **Wilde Writes** ~

25

Wilde writes with her eyes,
I am no poet. Just a witness.

She breathes lyrics and laughs harmonies.
Never has the movement of caressing hair
Behind
One's ear, been the muse of thy fingertips.

To touch,
To hold,
To feel with a being,
Who's aroma alone can ignite the
Ever-dark furnace in my chest.

Too accustomed to the emptiness my ribcage
Guarded,
I did not believe I would find you.

I wonder if you feel akin.
Do you?

You are by no means mine,
I don't think you ever will be,
Never completely.

Because you sore singularly.

A solo satellite, amongst the vastness.
Without company you are still composed.

I adore the buckle in your smile,
Tailing with each sarcastic remark.

It leaves you exposed.
I want to believe I see you true.

Such a bittersweetness you have left to linger on
My tongue.

I must warn you;
If you fall for a writer, be sure you're
Aware of some certainties;

All and any hurt,
I can,
I will hold from you.

Both the pleasure
& the pain we are bound to share
Will be chronicled,

Carved into the fabric being
Spun into my tapestry.

What is it about you?

You hold my grief and guilt-burdened gaze
As if it weighs no more than the air in our lungs.

The raw strength in your ocean eyes drowns me.
& I take pride in diving into your tide.

Will this seafarer be able to hold his breath,
Long enough to be brought back to life by your
Lips,
Once again?

~ **In The Dark. in the dark...** ~

I send you these words in the sweetness
Of the darkest hours
Long before the dawn.
You will wake,
Warm and well rested to
Turn and read what my my soul
Has let spill, with your divine sight.

I hope you wake and smile at these words,
At their meaning beyond their definitions.
I long to feel the radiance of your euphoric
Sigh
When you fall back into your sheets.

I say goodmorning to you when the rest say
Goodnight
Not because I wish for an unpleasant evening,
Only because I do not wish for a final memory
With you,
Only ever tomorrow.

~ **Those Twenty Can Wait** ~

Light begins to break when I wish you a
Goodnight.
Birds sing and scream and I
Know nothing of what they say.
Even knowing all the morning calls, I
Cannot fixate on another voice,
Like I do with yours.

" *I'm glad I met you* "
    " *I'm glad I met you too* "

It's hard to hold a necessity to sleep
When my wildest dreams and darkest of days
Hold a necessity to you.

I pray you find affirmation within these words.

I feel as if I am waking up to you.

~ **Sirens & Stained Mirrors** ~

It's far more intriguing to witness
Yourself in the reflection
Of the stained bar mirror.
But to deter my attention so easily,
There you are.

You are an entity I've never
Encountered before.
& it is unlikely I will be
Granted a subsequent encounter.

Your fire locks flow so elegantly that
Ballerinas dance in jealousy of
Their fluid immolating movements.

As much as you remind my subconscious of a
Mermaid,
Possibly a siren, though the
Differences do blur and blend together.
You handle too much dry to be convincing.

How come you can handle the land dwellers like
You do?

Yet why am I writing about people I
Know so little of?

Are we both so accustomed to
Appropriating the such we are not?

How can you force me to
Forget tomorrow so promiscuously?

~ The Truth She Speaks ~

I think I found another one
That cares.
The horror of it,
Such care is mirrored
In my heart.

"Goodnight x"

"Sleep well darling x
Thanks for the chat tonight.
It was fun"

"You too, yeah I enjoyed it x"

I love that you message me first.
You make me melt so meekly.
How do you create such miracles
Out of an apocalypse of a man?

You hid well from me,
Dressed in disguise,
I blame October.

My simple mind assumed
I could see who you are
Through your cinnamon skin but

I could never see all the spices
Within.
It's in the energy you possess,
The life you breathe out.

The truth you speak.

Miles have been travelled since the last
Memory, when I last felt this
Moved.

I will never forget the first time
You made me feel euphoria.
I rue for the man I met long ago
In the mirror,
A man that no longer resides
In my reflection,
he exists solely in the roots,
The soil and the poetry,

    Tattooed into pages,

        Carved into skin,

            Entangled under sheets.

~ **Why Do I Autumn?** ~

Why do you feel like Spring?
Your blooming smile amidst the blue
Dew drops eyes that roll off the petals of roses
Into my gaze.

Why do I feel like the last Autumn leaf?
Hanging on to my last leash of love,
When the wind blows in my defiance
& the rains do try to make me nothing
More than a wet papery annoyance
Between concrete and boot heels.

Am I hanging on,
Imitating an evergreen,
Determined to make it to Spring?
You remain out of reach,
The opposite to my fall,
Everything and nothing to me.

~ **Myself. The Child.** ~

Do you learn more or less
From your younger self as
Time tears you further apart
From the persons, you have lived as before.

Would you recognize the person you are
Today if you still saw yourself through the lens
Of
Such naivety?

The rose quartz glasses, we are born with.
We never take them off.
Never exchange them.
They age as we do and fade into existence
As a fraction of everything else, rather than
A separate entity entirely.

Some days you stumble, fall
For another, in the rhythmic disruption the
Glasses shift and your perspective with them.
You look through them with a slight difference
In angle,
In light
& unbeknownst you
There is an indistinguishable
Variance in the lens, where the fade has

Failed to corrupt completely.

You can see things as you started to.
You can be born again at that moment.
& the naivety returns.

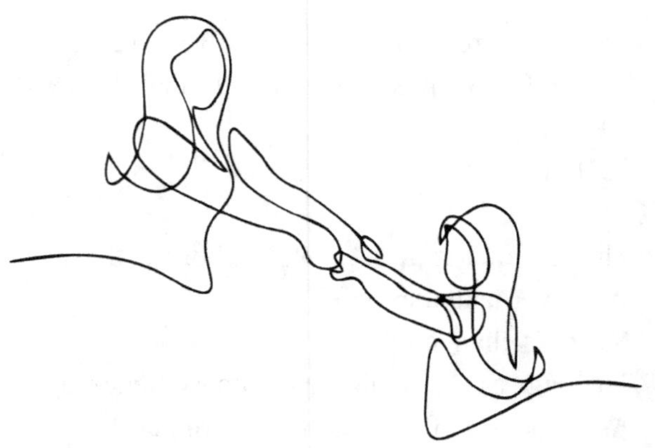

~ **How Can She Not Be French?** ~

He fears for her heart.
It is not fit,
Nor fair to break.

But how should he proceed?
Engage yourself, reader!
You are as much a part of this as the ink
& the trees
& the blood
& the bone marrow
Used to create this literary elixir.
So as you sip or scull,
Sink or swim.
Take these words, attempt a solution
For the dilemma He waltzed into.

Her body doesn't dance
the same.
Her lips taste of champagne
& not sunshine.
Yet her mind is a shot of espresso
That a day cannot be endured without.

Like others,
I witnessed the winds of Bordeaux
In her breath.

Perhaps born away from the motherland,
But French nonetheless.
Needless, I was wrong.

She however is only as french as I am
Which is none at all,
Until she rises from the sheets
Redressing with signature style,
Or the way her perceptions
Dispose of oppositions to beauty,
The way art calls her home.
How could I rid myself of such regality?

~ **Winter's Trees** ~

*"There's something incredibly honest about trees in winter,
how they're experts at letting things go"* – Jeffery McDaniel

In the bleak mid-winter, our goodbyes were
Wished
Away. I took the roots of our love and tore them
From health. Discarded the flowers and fruit,
She persists, lives and beautifies
The light for all to see.
While my thoughts and the fruits of them
Rot under the heat.

In the soil our seeds sowed a simple sweetness
Co-existed, beauty and trauma, bittersweet
Harmony.
In the polarise, we grew together, Then apart-
A life built together existed
In the complex constructs of our cortex
Conception.
A vivid dream that leaked into reality's lens.

That was our truth.
All that we were,
& all we were to be,
Existed irrespective of our poetic time and
Where we landed within this stanza.

Reality tortured our truth,
Turned dreams to nightmares,
& nightmares to fiction.
I always found more truth in fiction.

I know you didn't
You still don't.
Perhaps I'm still dreaming.

Perhaps I've grown content,
Living within a nightmare.

Perhaps it's time to wake.

9 789357 211659